Praise for MAKING CHOICES for the SUCCESSFUL ACTOR by Price Hall

"Price's method will change everything you've come to know about the art and craft of acting. He simplifies the work so that an actor can be truly present and let go of the planning and worrying about trying to get it right, both as an actor and in life. I am grateful for Price's willingness to give of himself to better us as actors and humans."

– Jameshia Bankston, Actress

"As a working actor, I have studied at the university level and with numerous highly qualified coaches. Price's method is an absolute paradigm shifter. I can finally achieve what has eluded me for years – being ME in the Work, unselfconsciousness, and in the moment."

– Joe DeMonico, Actor and Producer

"Studying with Price Hall has positively changed my direction both professionally and personally. His method is like a shot of the best actor's medicine. It puts you in the zone, just like reading this guide, a must-read for every actor."

— Terry Futschik, Actress

"The perfect carry-along for actors and performers. Making Choices has shown me the power of making unique choices in my work and of remaining in the moment. It will transform your career in TV and Film. A must-read for all actors."

— Chelsea Lee, Actress

"This guide brings us right to the heart of what it truly takes to become present in the moment. Anyone who absorbs the wisdom from these pages will be changed for the better, both professionally and on a deeply personal level."

— Christin Tolentino, Actress/Author

MAKING CHOICES for The SUCCESSFUL ACTOR

The Actor's Preparation Guide to Creative Character Development

Price Hall

Employee Millionaire

Paperback ISBN: 979-8-9879687-2-7

1st edition 2023

For information on bringing Price Hall to speak live at your event, please contact:

The Natural Act

281-910-0214

thenaturalact2@gmail.com

www.thenaturalact.net

To my dear friend and partner, Cathy, who was a true guide and who lived more in the moment than anyone I have ever known. Her memory keeps me Alive and Present and determined to stay true to my own spirit.

"From the ashes..."

Foreword by Malcolm McDowel

I don't have a lot of free time to read outside of the next script (got to work, work, work :-), so when Price Hall asked me to read his book, I figured I'd open it and be done with it a few minutes later. But, no, not the case here. Oh, no.

Not when Price starts off retelling the story of my first day on the set of his little gem of a film, ARTIST DIE BEST IN BLACK - now that's a title with teeth in it, unlike the one the Hollywood hacks chose for it (MISSISSIPPI MURDER). That was a really funny story, and truthful. I know...I was there.

Another reason I don't do many of these kinds of things is because - hush now - I'm no good at them. I'm all of over the place with this story and that story, and I forget all about the bloody reason I am writing this Foreword in the first place. It's not about me telling stories (which I have been doing my entire working life), but... well, I wanted to do this one because MAKING CHOICES is unique and different.

MAKING CHOICES is just what we do in life, every second of every day, so why shouldn't we break it down, the way Price has done in his brilliant little guidebook - by the way, did I tell you I think its brilliant? - and provide actors a direct, logical, and simple way - Price calls it a Handle...Brilliant! - to get inside the character and the situation, and then just listen and respond naturally. It's BRILLIANT! (Love that word.)

But to be frank, I knew everything about Price Hall (as a coach) by the way he directed his film on that first day I was on the set. Kind, (dare I say, brill...no, I won't say it) smart, answered every question an actor could think of about the character, kept on schedule without making us (the actors) feel rushed, had me fall/jump out of a 2-story window into a pile of cardboard box's on the paved driveway below (Oh yes, I die in the movie - spoiler :-)...Actually, it was a pair of brave stuntmen who took the spill...reminds me of a scene a few years before in A CLOCKWORK ORANGE...another story for another day.

I told Price back then, that if he had only directed his film 10 years earlier, he would have 9 more films under his belt by then and a brilliant (oooh, that word) career already. Well, maybe this is why he didn't go that route.

Instead, he has squeezed the true essence out of the craft of acting and distilled it down into MAKING CHOICES.

Thank you for the opportunity to read this guidebook and make comments on it. Working with Price Hall as a director was a truly memorable experience. I know that any actor, newbie or credited thespian, will benefit tremendously by reading MAK-ING CHOICES.

In fact, given that the information in the book is about what makes humans tick, it's a read I would, and will, recommend for any human beings who want to get more out of their life.

Brilliant!

Malcolm McDowel

Actor, Producer, and Television Presenter

Contents

Introduction

I WAS BORN AND raised in Richmond, Virginia, and got my first taste of show biz somewhere around the age of 10 when I was double-cast as a kid and a rat in the stage production of THE PIED PIPER. I absolutely loved life until the first dress rehearsal, when I discovered I would need to transform from the kid to the rat in the same backstage changing area as the little girls/sister rats. Until that moment, I didn't know I could run so fast.

Thank goodness that over-exaggerated experience did not keep me away from the world of performing, and eventually from the world of teaching, coaching, and directing actors, which I have developed a deep passion for. So much so, that I have now been doing it for over 30 years, have founded and run my own entertainment teaching/coaching and consulting company, The Natural Act, have directed one full-length feature film, and am poised to direct my second.

It's been a great, albeit challenging Life, but one which I would not trade. Especially for the opportunities I have had to work with amazing human beings, both as teachers and fellow performers. It is out of those opportunities and experiences that I have discovered the true beauty of humanity, and what I believe is a desire on the part of most humans to have that primary experience of expressing their innermost selves through a Craft such as Acting, or at the least, as audience members vicariously experiencing it through those actors on stage or screen.

While there are numerous philosophies on the best way to master the Craft of Acting, at the end of the day, they are all dealing with something ephemeral and intangible, and are all the products of someone's opinion.

All of the information you will be exposed to here is also only someone's opinion—my own. Study and put into practice as many of these philosophies as you care to experience or feel are valuable, but your ultimate goal should be to discover and develop your own method, your own unique approach.

It is a journey of **SELF**-discovery.

Welcome To It!

PRICE HALL | The Natural Act

Chapter One

The Set Up

WHY THIS GUIDE BOOK? I would have to say it's the culmination of all of my years of working and studying as an Actor, my years of teaching and coaching Actors, and all of it coming together in one particular moment when I was directing my first full-length feature film, called at the time, *ARTISTS DIE BEST IN BLACK*. It has since been renamed *MISSISSIPPI MURDER* by the Hollywood distribution company that picked it up. Hollywood...LOL.

Before the film, I had developed numerous workshops on the art and craft of acting for the camera and had the idea that what made an actor watchable on-screen and desirable for a director to hire was something called ***Presence***, or ***Being Here Now***. And this I found was opposed to, but not necessarily exclusive of, being a good actor. It was simply that in trying to act well, one's focus, it seemed, was on 'doing it right', as opposed to simply 'being in the work'.

This 'doing it right' constituted a desire for the actor to please others and to care about what others thought about the actor's work. It was this 'caring' that diminished the **Presence** in the actor's work. So, it became my opinion that the best an actor could do for themselves was to kill 'caring'.

> ### *The best an actor could do for themselves was to kill 'caring'.*

It was one of those extremely hot and muggy summer days in mid-July on the Mississippi Gulf Coast. The shelf life for anything breathing, without air conditioning, was not worth considering. And it was the day we were shooting the fighting and death scene of one of my movie's lead actors and a young, brilliant up-and-comer. The characters in the movie were meant to have a deep history with each other, whereas the actors were meeting for the very first time when they stepped on the set that day. It's one of the reasons they call it *acting*.

The scene was being shot in an upstairs library of one of those gorgeous, old seaside Mississippi mansions, which for some unknown and unfathomable reason, had no central air conditioning. So, we had A/C tubes snaking throughout the home providing the hard-working crew with the life-giving 'cool' necessary to keep moving and breathing. But, come time to actually begin shooting the scene, all machinery would need to be shut down because of the sound recording issues, which included that oh-so-cool air conditioning.

This meant we would need to shoot fast and efficiently so that our actors, and their make-up, would survive the muggy heat. And again, this was one of our lead actors, and it was his first day in the film. The last thing I wanted to do was start off on the wrong foot with one of the people who would eventually help get our film sold. If I had known Malcolm McDowell before that day, I would not have been worried, because as it turns out, he does not have a 'wrong' foot. I guess that comes from years of working under every conceivable kind of condition, and from being a British gentleman.

Endeavoring to be a brilliant, well-oiled machine that could get the needed footage for this very important piece of our story in as little time as possible, we did camera rehearsal after camera rehearsal until we felt confident in our choreography. When I finally called 'Action', everything would simply 'click' and the actors would never even know the A/C had been off.

And then, my brilliant young actor, Chris, stepped onto the set, brimming over with enthusiasm and zeal, and began regaling me with a non-stop recanting of his preparation for his character and his plans for the scene. Amid this oration, Malcolm entered the room, and like a character from a Shakespearean play, announced, "Ready!"

Without a break in his enthusiasm, Chris turned on his heel and bee-lined it for Malcolm, where he continued the non-stop narration of his preparation and plans for the scene. He did deviate long enough to humbly introduce himself. In the middle of this friendly onslaught, Malcolm looked over Chris' shoulder, locked eyes with me, and said, "Price, can we just shoot the bloody scene!"

At that moment, it became crystal clear to me that all of our rehearsals and choreography were going straight out the window because here was an actor who trusted himself enough not to need to know what was coming next, or how to do anything. It was clear that what he loved about the Craft of Acting was NOT knowing, but instead, *exploring* the possibilities of every moment...just like Life.

So, I yelled to the crew, "Forget everything we've rehearsed. Get the steady-cam operator, and we'll just follow the action."

Freaked out, the rug having just been pulled from beneath his feet, Chris rushed up to me and said, "You can't do this. What about all of my preparation, everything I've planned?"

I looked him straight in the eyes, where I saw something akin to a mixture of terror and threat, smiled and patted him on his shoulder, and said, "Roll with it", then turned to the room and called, "Places".

By the time we had finished shooting the scene, everyone on the crew, including myself, and the actors, were all laughing from the exhilarating experience we had just had. It was clearly the most energetic and lively piece of the film we had yet shot, and everyone was clear it was the most exciting.

We had just been involved with **being in the work**, as opposed to *doing the work* in a particular way, the way we had rehearsed it. Because of Malcolm, we had let ourselves be Free to film the scene as it created itself.

We were in the Moment. Present. We were all reveling in our aliveness.

And best of all, Chris absolutely loved it.

Thank you, Chris, for being courageous enough to 'roll with it', and to you, Malcolm, for inspiring us all to deal with and revel in our fear of *Being Present*.

Chapter Two

Which One Are You?

HAVE YOU EVER FOUND yourself sitting in a theater watching the actors on the screen and saying to yourself, "Man, would I love to be doing that!"? Then the movie ends, and you walk outside and back into your normal life. And, that's as far as it goes. Until the next film or the next television show, and that gnawing feeling comes back, just as strong as ever, and you're wishing once again it could be you up on that screen. You might even have found yourself going a step further and saying, "Heck, I could do that." And maybe you could.

Or...

Have you been out there for a while? You've got an agent, and every so often they call or email you with an audition. It happened yesterday. It's not a great role, but hey, it would be working as an actor, not a legal assistant which you do to pay the bills. So, you put your time in, learning your lines and working on the character. The day comes, and you get up early to drive the 2 and-a-half hours to where the audition is being held, you walk in, ready to knock 'em alive, and you wind up with a reader who sleepwalks through the entire scene. Your 2.5-hour drive of excitement and anticipation there turns into a forever journey of disappointment and frustration going home.

Or...

*H*ave you just finished shooting and editing the self-taped audition for the low-budget indie that's shooting in one of those tax-incentivized states (your third self-taped audition this week)? Actually, you decided to elevate the quality of your audition this time so that it would stand out from the rest for once. So, you paid a cameraman to shoot and edit it for you, and it only cost $150. Ouch! You check out the finished product once more before hitting *SEND*, and for the very first time, you notice how many times you licked your lips. OMG! Well, maybe they won't catch it. Maybe.

Or...

Are you seasoned? You've been working. You could always work more, but you're building your name and your brand. The roles you're landing are pretty decent, but... The truth is, it all feels the same. Repeating lines, and hitting your mark. Being challenged in the work is the last thing you feel. You've gotten comfortable.

The reason you got into this business in the first place is that the work was like the best drug you could ever take. It was all of *You, Passionately Alive*! *Present*! You want that again.

Or...

Send in your version of how you began and where you are in the pursuit of your dream or goals as an actor. We want to know. Look for The Natural Act contact info in the back.

Chapter Three

What Gets You There?

WHETHER YOU'RE AT THE very beginning of your pursuit of this thing called '*acting*', or you've made a clear and definitive choice that '*acting*' is your life, it is ultimately important to understand that '*acting*' is a craft. Meaning you can't just fall out of bed and say, "I am an actor". Although, that's not necessarily a bad place to start. In fact, any place is a good place to start, as long as that first 'step' is followed by another.

What's important is your '*follow through*'.

And just how much *follow-through*, translating into time and hard work, is necessary before you can begin to enjoy the fruits of your impassioned labor? That truly depends on you. But, after having been in the entertainment industry for over 30 years, it is my educated and experienced opinion that...

It is not so much how much time you invest in building a craft. It is, instead, how you approach building it.

*If you set out to cross the Sahara Desert, and you're told it will take you a month to do so on foot, and you begin walking, it is probably going to take you a month. But, if your true **NEED** is simply to get to the other side of the desert, then why not hop a ride on that camel over there? Better yet, how about that Range Rover that's about to depart with some very interesting traveling companions and an ice chest filled with poached salmon and cold champagne? Oh, and the Rover has a Bose surround-sound system and touchscreen climate control.*

There is NO absolute, proven method or approach to becoming a professional, working *actor*. One day you aren't, and the next day you are. This actually says a lot about individuals who make the decision to become *actors*...mainly that they can live with uncertainty and they can roll with the punches. You must have that kind of resiliency in your psyche and soul, and you must be absolutely passionate about the *work*... the *craft*.

It is that passion that will continue to drive you, and that resiliency that will get you through the challenging times, however much time that may be.

And, if your **NEED** is to become a good, working actor, it really may not be a function of time at all. It may instead be a function of efficiency, and **a *way* to remain immersed in that passion**...

...A ***Clear*, *Simple*,** and ***Specific* 'HANDLE'** that gets you to the core of the work each and every time you work.

MAKING CHOICES for the Successful Actor will provide you with that **HANDLE**.

Chapter Four

The What

ACTOR: "What does it really take to become a successful, working Actor?"

COACH: "If I had to answer that question in two simple words, they would be...***NO FEAR***."

ACTOR: "How does one get to a place of NO FEAR?"

COACH: "By being confident in your ability to deliver whatever is required for the role on cue, time and time again...without caring what anybody thinks of you in the process."

ACTOR: "Sounds simple."

COACH: "It is...but easy, it's not."

ACTOR: "Is there a clear, logical way to get to that place, that doesn't require years and years of study?"

COACH: "Yes."

That's what **MAKING CHOICES** is all about.

Coach's Note

HAVE YOU EVER COMPARED the way that actors on the screen behave... with real people you observe on a day-to-day basis? If your answer is 'No', then consider this your first homework, or more to the point, your first *Life*-work assignment. Because...

> **Life-Work:** The ongoing observation & study of humanity and all Life Living outside of you.

All good 'Acting' is just like Life... or better yet, a heightened sense of Life. One where you become keenly aware of the nature of what we humans call *Being* Alive, which, for the purpose of this dialectic, translated for the Actor, means... **Being Present**.

Presence is the state we as actors strive to experience in our work, because...

Presence is the doorway that leads us to... NO FEAR.

Challenge ONE

To act well, which means acting truthfully, which means being present and in the moment, requires us first, to be in a state of observance. In general, the observance of the world around us, and not the observance of ourselves in the world.

Make a trip to a nearby grocery store. From the moment you arrive, expand and extend your powers of observation. Become keenly aware of the human beings who are there along with you... and not just the customers, but the employees as well.

Observe what they are wearing, and see if that tells you anything about the kind of humans they are. Or the items they throw in their basket. Or the way the employees stack items on the shelves. Look for behaviors, ticks, the interactions between shoppers, or employees. Notice anything that catches your sensibility, anything that stands out as superbly human. And watch for those almost hidden aspects of their humanity. You may just find that it is the little things that make us the most human.

Notice these things. Write them down or record them in some other fashion only if you choose to. There is no requirement on my part for you to do anything other than *observe*.

This is not a test you can fail. In fact, you can consider this entire guide an easy pass.

Be Interested. Observe. Grow.

Challenge TWO

To be Observant of the world around you, which allows you to act well, without **FEAR**, a lack of **SELF**-Consciousness is required. And **SELF**-Consciousness is a direct function of where your Attention is Focused.

Wherever you are right this minute (assuming you are not involved in some activity that requires your full focus or attention... such as driving, operating dangerous equipment, or rock climbing at Yosemite... you get the picture) take 30 seconds and focus your full attention on your-**SELF**.

Ready...

ACTION...

Tick-tock...

CUT.

How'd that go? Did you succeed? Ok, great.

Now, here we go again. This time, locate an object or another person, take another 30 seconds, and focus your full attention there.

Ready...

ACTION...

Tick-tock...

CUT.

How about that? Did you succeed? Great.

Now, one last time, take 30 seconds and focus your full attention on your-*SELF*, and at exactly the same time, focus your full attention on the object or person you were focused on a moment ago.

You got that? Ok, great.

Here we go...and...

ACTION...

Tick-tock...

CUT.

How did that go? Did you succeed? Be honest, now.

NO! You did *NOT* succeed!

It is not possible to focus your full attention in more than one direction at a time.

Again, your FULL ATTENTION!

You may be able to focus fragmented attention in more than one direction at a time, you multi-tasker you, but not your full attention! And to...

Act Well, with NO FEAR, you must have your FULL ATTENTION Focused OUTSIDE OF YOUR-SELF.

This creates the state of *being present...* of **PRESENCE.**

And from the second challenge you've just completed, you can see that where you focus your attention is totally up to you. You can **choose** where your attention is going to be focused. Meaning...

*You can **choose** NOT to be **SELF**-CONSCIOUS.*

*You can **choose** to have **NO FEAR**.*

*It's your **Choice**.*

Chapter Five

Fear

YOU CAN TRULY ONLY act well with *NO FEAR*.

Because *FEAR* is all about you...

- *FEAR* of not doing well

- *FEAR* of not remembering the lines

- *FEAR* of not remembering how to say that line the way you rehearsed all those times

- *FEAR* of not looking good

- *FEAR* of being judged by the casting director or director

- *FEAR* of not getting the job

- *FEAR* of doing such a bad job in the audition that you will never be asked to audition again

- *FEAR* of being *FEAR*ful, for Pete's sake!

FEAR only exists when your attention is focused on your-*SELF*.

FEAR is the killer of *Presence* and the *Dr. Fronkenschteen* (HA!) of *SELF*-CONSCIOUSNESS!

You've Heard This One...

You've **heard** the story at some point in your life about a person who lifted a car off of someone who was being crushed beneath it.

Do you really think that person stopped to consider if they were strong enough to pull that off before they did it?... Maybe they were *FEARful* they couldn't do it, but then decided to go ahead, and succeeded anyway?

Not likely!

What is likely is that the person never had a thought for themselves, of whether or not they might fail. They only had their attention focused on the person beneath that hunk of steel or fiberglass, or whatever the vehicle was made of, and on seeing that they were OK.

Their attention was fully focused outside of themselves, generating a state of **NO SELF**-Consciousness, of **NO FEAR**, which allowed that normal human being to pull off a superhuman feat.

And do you think they were surprised afterward, or could even remember what they had just done? My guess is YES they were surprised, and NO, they had no clear memory of what they had just done!

Chapter Six

The Handle

FEAR SEPARATES YOU FROM the world and those around you! And **SELF**-Consciousness is the breeding ground for **FEAR**. It separates you from the other *actor* or *actors* you are acting with. It prevents you from *being present*, *being in the moment*, because the moment exists exactly mid-way between you and the other *actor*, where your attentions collide, where they **NEED** to meet, and where you dance together in this thing called a *scene*, which I will refer to simply from this point forward, as...

... a ***Conversation***. Kind of like the format of this guide.

The *characters* don't have a clue they are doing a *scene*. Only the *actors* know this. And while the *actor* and the *character* are the same person, meaning *'you'*, you are never both at the same time.

The *actor prepares* the *scene*, but the *character lives*, moment by moment, in a *conversation*, with no beginning, middle, or end, speaking *conversationally*, not spouting lines written for an actor to say.

The only time that exists for the *character* is *'now'*. Just like you. In real life. Because remember... Acting is just like life.

So, if **NO FEAR** is the desired state for you, the actor, and not being **SELF**-Conscious is the way to achieve that state, then why not just do that? If you can actually **choose** whether or not you will be conscious of your-**SELF**, why not just do that and have it over with?

Because... it's a bit easier said than done!

I hate that.

Seriously, if you can achieve that state of **NO FEAR** every time you work, flying by the seat of your pants, or if like the Irish on this St. Patrick's Day, which I am spending in the wild and crazy, and totally *un-SELF Conscious* city of New Orleans, you can just luckily pull it off every time you work, then more power to you.

The more likely reality you will find, as I have, of putting this approach into action so that you can come to depend upon it each and every time you work, is that you will **NEED** to treat it like a sport. To become adept at it, you will work on some aspects of it daily, so that eventually you don't need to think about it when you work.

It becomes your *Way*, and your *Way* becomes you.

> **The Handle:** A universal tool that will serve you, the actor, in any situation where ***NO FEAR*** is desired and required.

It is The ***HANDLE*** that you can depend upon no matter what the situation.

You play tennis... do you want to play at Wimbledon? You've got to swing that racquet more than just a few times. You're an actor, and you want to play up on the big or little screen?

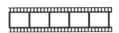

HERE'S _HOW_...

Chapter Seven

The How

So now that you have a clear understanding of **What** I am talking about, let's build off of that, and get down to **How** to put this...

Clear!...Simple!...Specific!

...approach to the *work* in your work.

There are **Six Specific Points** that you must identify for your-***SELF*** as the *actor* before you can actually, fully step into the *character*.

But, even before that occurs, there is a very basic, logical action you MUST accomplish:

READ and ***UNDERSTAND*** the *conversation* so that you have a clear understanding of the genre and emotional content (dramatic, comedic, tragic, mystery, thriller, horror, etc.) and the *nature* of your *character* (good person, bad person, etc.) in the story.

Seems logical, I know, but you would be surprised how many actors just jump right in without having made these necessary determinations. They are so excited about having an opportunity to play a character that they simply jump off the cliff forgetting that they forgot their wings. They quickly find out that you really can't fly by the seat of your pants. And this is quite different from sailing off the cliff with the right tools and equipment and building your wings on the way down.

Quickly...***QUICKLY!***

So, here we go.

POINT ONE: WHO Are You?

Meaning, Who are you as the Character?

If I were to ask you who you are, and I mean who you are in real life, you would probably be able to carry on for some time telling me all about yourself:

- Your name

- Where you grew up

-

Who your parents are, if they are still together, still living, how they treated you growing up

- If you have siblings and what those relationships were/are like

- If you live in a house or apartment

- If you drive a car, ride a bike, or take public transportation

- If you have a dog or a cat or a hamster or a goldfish or a parrot or a turtle

- If you had or have money or have struggled your entire life

- If you're married or divorced, have a lover, or are sworn to celibacy for life

- If you are successful or not there yet

- And on and on...

The more you define and describe your-**SELF**, the more you find to say about your-**SELF**. This is the kind of understanding you must bring to your character, that helps you define the *nature* of your character.

The difference here is...

You get to use your *creative imagination*.

You get to create the *You* that is the '*tastiest You*' you can imagine, the '*tastiest You*' that you could possibly want to play as a character, and you build that *You* from the ground up, all based upon the *nature* of your character in the story, as you understand it.

And even better, no one can tell you that you are wrong about the **YOU** you create, because that's your secret. How many people in your real life do you divulge every aspect of who you are to? Simply, you are a walking, talking exhibit of who you are.

What you see is what you get.

Well, not always, right? But, that's part of you too.

You are your secret, and so is your character.

Coach's <u>BIG</u> Note

The Make Yourself RIGHT Factor (MYR)

As regards *character*, you are creating yourself as the best, the *'tastiest You'* your creative imagination can come up with, which remains your secret.

It stays in the background.

Meaning, no one is going to be able to tell you if you're right or if you're wrong. So, don't question yourself, because you cannot play a *maybe*. Make yourself right!

> **MYR:** Make your-*SELF* Right! Satisfy your-*SELF* 1st. *Make* the *Choice* that works for you. This is your Secret.

100%! Never doubt your amazing creative imagination!

The great thing about this part of the process is, once you create an element like *who you are as the character*, you do not have to try and remember it. It is part of your *preparation*, and unlike the lines, you must learn and remember, once you have done this *preparation*, it is automatically in place for you to draw upon.

You might be thinking: Just like that?

Yes, just like that.

An analogy will help you understand how and why *preparation* works this way. Keep reading. It's coming.

For this to be its most effective, its most indelible, you should commit it to the written word... Not on a computer or mobile device. Write it out by hand.

This makes a deeper impression, a clearer mind-emotion connection than modern technology can't provide. And since you act the most effectively from your gut and your heart, not your brain, you can understand how *important* that mind-emotion connection is.

POINT TWO: What's the RELATIONSHIP?

Meaning the **relationship** between you and the other *character* or *characters* you are in *conversation* with.

Are they your:

- brother or sister

- mother or father

- wife or husband

- boyfriend or girlfriend

- doctor or patient

- dog-catcher or animal rights activist

- President or Dictator

- are you strangers

- are you enemies

- and on and on

That's all fairly straightforward stuff, and most often will either be crystal clear or stated in the *conversation* or description itself.

But equally, or even more important, is the *nature* and *quality* of the relationship: how you relate to the other character physically, emotionally, psychologically, and spiritually. The nuances and dynamics that will generate.

Here's what I mean:

You are brother and sister in the scene. Fine, in that you are blood relatives, and that bespeaks a certain familiarity, *BUT*...

- is it a loving or a bitter familiarity?

- is one of you gay and one straight?

- did one of you abuse the other growing up?

- has one of you got a crime in your background that the other knows about but has never divulged?

This information is almost never made clear in the dialogue or description of the *conversation*. It will likely be found *only* in the deep and sometimes chillingly dark or hilariously ridiculous recesses of your *creative imagination*.

And this is where the real *FUN* begins!

You make up, you create the person you would most like to play as the character, and no one can tell you it is wrong. They also cannot tell you if it's right. Because all of this information is your secret unless you choose to share it with someone... the director for example.

This *preparation* is the real work of the actor, where they can reach deep inside their psyches and pull out aspects of humanity that fascinate them, and then give birth to that particular human being and live in their skin from their first step to the end of their imaginary and purposeful existence.

Remember **MYR**!

The reality is, the actor actually becomes an unlicensed behavioral psychologist. Unless of course, you actually are a licensed behavioral psychologist...HA!

Remember your first *life assignment*: Observe the behavior of real people on a day-to-day basis.

This speaks to one of the wonderful social benefits Actors can give to their fellow humans, that of illuminating the human condition through their work, and in so doing, providing the much-needed service of allowing your audience to experience *their* own emotions, *their* own lives, vicariously through you, the Character. So, to serve your purpose the most effectively, you must become the best unlicensed behavioral psychologist possible so the audience can 'enjoy' their own humanity to the greatest degree. And when you have truly become adept at doing that, you sometimes wind up...

ACTOR (grins): "Winning an Oscar?"

COACH: "How about...getting the job?"

BACK TO **RELATIONSHIP.** IT is truly the nuances, the dynamic, that creates the most interesting characters, the undercurrents that play beneath the skin, the questions and emotions that swim behind the eyes, that create that *Inner Life* the camera, the director, and the audience long to see, long to be '*hooked*' by.

The *relationship* in your *conversation* is that you are married. That's all the *conversation* gives you.

Could be pretty normal, pretty boring, or off-the-charts dangerous.

Take a look...

Scene 1, Take 1

INT. KITCHEN - NIGHT

ELLEN LEANS AGAINST THE island, a half-full glass of wine in her hands. Two smoldering pots sit on the burners of the range behind her. Chopping board, gleaming carving knife, and sliced tomatoes. Places are set at the table, plates full, and one full glass of wine.

Ellen stares out the window. Tears stain her cheeks.

She hears the front door slam. Wipes the tears away with her sleeve.

John casually walks in, stumbles over the rug, and catches himself.

JOHN *(slurs to himself)*: "Stupid rug..."

Ellen looks up at the clock over the window. Reads 9:45. Then back to John.

ELLEN: "Dinner was ready an hour ago."

John straightens himself up.

JOHN: "Oh, yeah, sorry. Had a flat."

He holds up two overly dirty hands.

ELLEN: "You think about calling?"

John hangs onto the counter, supporting himself.

They lock eyes.

JOHN: "Phone died."

Ellen glares at him, finishes off her glass of wine, and sets it on the counter.

She walks past John toward the door.

ELLEN: "Clean up when you're done."

She's gone. John stares at the knife on the cutting board.

SUB-Story / SUB-Text

Definitely not a happy, married couple, at least not at this particular moment. And that is probably how most Actors would approach the *Conversation*, playing for the emotion of anger. And why not? John was late, he didn't find a way to let Ellen know, she put effort into preparing a nice dinner for the two of them, and now it's ruined. And she's pissed. And he's pissed because she's pissed. Just like life. HA! End of story.

COACH: "Not really...No, not at all."

If you explore the possibilities in their *relationship* for the nuances, the dynamics, the **SUB**-story, which in turn creates the **SUB**-text, which provides the *actor* with those questions, those words left unspoken behind the eyes, it *naturally* creates that brilliant Inner Life.

Here's another expanded look at the same *Conversation*, with specific lines of **SUB**-text inserted parenthetically. This **SUB**-text is given by a particular **SUB**-story, which you, the Actor, create with that wonderful *creative imagination* you so long to unleash.

COACH

And don't forget **MYR (MAKE YOURSELF RIGHT – 100%)!**

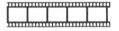

THE *SUB*-STORY:

John and Ellen's marriage is going bad, and John is having an affair. Ellen suspects.

Scene 1, Take 2

INT. KITCHEN - NIGHT

Ellen leans against the island, a half-full glass of wine in her hands (this is her second glass, and she's feeling it). Two smoldering pots sit on the burners of the range behind her. Chop-ping board, gleaming carving knife, and sliced tomatoes. Places are set at the table, plates full, and one full glass of wine.

Ellen stares out the window. Tears stain her cheeks. (He'll come in late again, with another lame excuse. I can't take this much longer.)

She hears the front door slam. Wipes the tears away with her sleeve. (I won't give him the pleasure of knowing that I know about her, and how much it destroys me.)

John casually walks in, stumbles over the rug, and catches himself. (He's had a few, which he needs to be able to walk back into this house, into this marriage that doesn't work anymore.)

JOHN *(slurs to himself)*: "Stupid rug..."

Ellen looks up at the clock over the window. Reads 9:45. Then back to John. (He feels her eyes on him, her suspicions.)

ELLEN: "Dinner was ready an hour ago."

John straightens himself up. (Ok, here I go. Doesn't she get how much I hate this, hate myself for doing this, hate her.)

JOHN: "Oh, yeah, sorry. Had a flat."

He holds up two overly dirty hands. (I know she doesn't buy this. Why doesn't she say something about it...call me on it?)

(He must think I'm an idiot. I know he's lying. He's been with her.)

ELLEN: "You think about calling?"

John hangs onto the counter, supporting himself.

They lock eyes. (Is this the moment when we both finally tell the truth?)

JOHN: "Phone died."

Ellen glares at him, (Bastard!) finishes off her glass of wine, and sets it on the counter.

She walks past John toward the door. (I'm calling my attorney in the morning.)

ELLEN: "Clean up when you're done."

She's gone. John stares at the knife on the cutting board. (Oh, I'll clean up all right.)

TAKE 1 AND TAKE 2 are written exactly the same, except for the parenthetical **SUB**-text, which you have added. But, the *conversations* are totally different because of the **SUB**-story about the *relationship* which is not on the page. You, the actor, have created and provided a much tastier *relationship* using your *creative imagination*, which I will suggest, would be a more interesting, exciting *conversation* to have, other than simply satisfying the emotion in the lines by just being mad at each other.

The **SUB**-story of John cheating on Ellen provides nuance, a dynamic, and energy simply by weaving that into their *relationship*, and logically gives birth to Your **SUB**-text. You don't have to do anything to the lines or yourself, other than focus your full attention on the other character, and...

COACH: "...Let the words fall out of your mouth."

And because we are talking about the *relationship*, it also makes sense that we are talking about, and *to*, someone in particular, right? A relationship between a wife and a husband is very different from a relationship between, for example, an employer and an employee. Specifically, who you are to each other would most likely be spelled out in the description or on the page. But, as we've seen, the dynamic and nuances of that *relationship* are truly the domain of the actor's *creative imagination* and the fallout from the **SUB**-story.

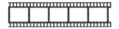

PEOPLING...GOTCHA!

There is one more layer in the *relationship*, another **'Gotcha'** you, the actor, does to you, the *character*, which may very well provide the deepest emotional connection of all. And this is definitely *NOT* on the page.

COACH: "Here we go again...**MYR.**"

Let's go back to our unhappily married couple, John and Ellen. You are auditioning for one of the roles, and you're preparing with my assistance.

The first thing I ask you is:

PRICE: "**Who** Are you as the *character*?"

Then I ask you:

PRICE: "What's the **Relationship**?"

For the sake of this little drill, I'm working with Alan who is reading for JOHN.

PRICE: "So, Alan, let's establish the relationship. Who is Ellen?"

ALAN: "My wife...John's wife."

PRICE: "Right. But, who is she?"

ALAN: "I told you. She's my wife."

PRICE: "Ok. But, who is she to *you*, really?"

ALAN: "I've been married to her for 11 years and I have had it."

PRICE: "So, obviously she is not your favorite person at this moment, right?"

ALAN: "You can say that again."

PRICE: "If you were to describe her and how you feel about her, what would you say?"

ALAN: "She's a total nag, never gives me a moment's peace, and I'd be happy to never see her again."

PRICE: " So, strong opinions and feelings about her?"

ALAN: "Oh yeah."

PRICE: "She reminds you of anybody in your life, Alan?"

Alan pauses and thinks. Connects. His eyes blaze.

ALAN: "HA!... Yep, my first wife's mother!"

PRICE: "So, if your former mother-in-law were to walk through the door right now, and you were to turn and see her, how would you feel?"

ALAN: "Oh boy, I'd wanta..."

Alan's real anger stops him as he thinks about her.

PRICE: "So, look at the door, use your imagination, and see her walk into the room. But, don't just think about her...really see her. See what she's wearing, see the look in her eyes..."

Alan looks at the door, and takes a moment, his eyes narrow...steam wafts out of his ears.

PRICE: "You see her, don't you?"

Alan, his eyes still glued to the door.

ALAN: "Oh yeah. Smell her too. That damn perfume.

PRICE: "Ok. Now, just tell her, 'Sorry, had a flat.'"

ALAN *(through gritted teeth, murderous)*: "Sorry, had a flat."

Alan remains fixed on the door.

PRICE: "Ok, Alan. Let it go."

Alan's face relaxes. Rubs his eyes.

ALAN *(laughs out loud)*: "Man, that was intense!"

PRICE: "Yes. And that was Ellen, your wife."

What Alan just experienced is what I call '***Peopling***' the scene. Another term you may have heard for this process is substitution. 'Peopling' seems to me a more humanistic term, and given we as actors are out to stimulate the actual emotions of humans, of our audiences, peopling hits the bulls-eye with a bit more feeling.

> **PEOPLING:** Using your imagination to create, in real-time, people from your life who generate real, specific emotions which are carried over into your work.

Simply, it's using your *creative imagination* to generate truthful emotion for the Work by seeing and experiencing in real-time, not just thinking about and remembering, people in your own personal life that have you *Feel* a clear and specific emotion. An emotion you can count on, take after take.

And then using those people that are real to you, that are familiar to you, instead of an actor you may have just met for the first time in your life. Or, a bored reader, to have you truthfully feel the way You, the Character, **NEEDS** to feel in the *conversation*.

If you explore the possible people from your life to use for 'Peopling', meaning you spend time seeing them, creating them out of thin air, so to speak, you will realize which ones do stimulate real emotion and which ones leave you exhausted from trying too hard. Identify which emotions, specifically, the winners you have experienced truthfully, not once, but at least several times, then create a List. This List of at least 5-10 people (could also be non-humans...does your Goldfish have you laugh hysterically?) will be your...

Peopling Cheat Sheet (Example)

WHO	HOW YOU SEE THEM	EMOTION
Nancy	In her blue dress	Deep Love
Fred	Tennis shorts & shirt	Happiness
Johann	Blue Business suit	Dis-trust
Alicia	Pink warm-up suit	Sadness
Scott	Jeans & tee-shirt	Hatred
Barney (your goldfish)	Orange, scaly skin, open mouth	Hilarious Laughter

The List should cover the entire range of emotions you will ever need to call into action. All you will need to do is determine which emotion the *conversation* requires, scroll down your cheat sheet, find the appropriate human (or fish)...

COACH: "...Plug them in, and you're good to go."

And to get you started, below, fill in the blanks on your own **Peopling Cheat Sheet.**

FIND A QUIET PLACE to sit, alone. Decide on an emotion, either close your eyes or leave them open (eventually you will need to work with your eyes open), and see who shows up. Or, if you are clear about a person and *how* they make you feel, see them first and see if you actually experience that specific emotion. You may be surprised to find that you don't feel that emotion, or you don't feel it strongly enough, or you feel nothing at all. Don't push your-**SELF** to feel something if you don't. This is an exploration. Enjoy the journey!

Your Peopling Cheat Sheet

WHO	HOW YOU SEE THEM	EMOTION

Coach's Note

Just because you have created your **Peopling Cheat Sheet**, does not mean it's plug-and-play. This, like so many other aspects of the *work*, requires regular practice. Like a sport, you only become adept after many long hours of dedicated effort. Hours that allow you at some point, to own your *craft*, without having to think about the 'how' of it. To become your '*way*'. Or better put, for the '*way*' to become you.

It becomes an effortless process, as the process for all '*good*' Acting is. Instead of trying to 'do' something, trying to make something *happen*, you simply have to provide your-**SELF** with the appropriate stimulus and 'allow' it to act upon you. *To be present... In the Moment.* Without being concerned about whether or not you are succeeding, whether or not you are doing it right, whether or not anybody likes you, whether or not you get the call-back or the job. All of that is about '*you*', you thinking about '*you*', and you being concerned about '*you.*' You being **SELF**-Conscious.

COACH: "That is Acting. *B-A-A-A-A-D*!

The Goal is simply, to **Be**,...

...With **NO FEAR**."

POINT THREE: What's The Situation?

Meaning literally, what's *Happening* in the *conversation*?

So, you've read and now you understand the *conversation*.

COACH: "*Conversation* is the new reference for 'scene', remember?"

You know who you are as the *character*, and you are clear about the *relationship* and its *dynamic, nature,* and *quality*. All of this helps create Nuance that plays beneath the text (**SUB**-text) and swims behind the eyes to generate an Inner Life. This too, is possible, and desirable, in the Situation.

But, if the *situation* is simply what's happening in the *conversation*, that seems pretty straightforward. It's black and white. Where is the *nuance* in that? Again, it requires the use of that unique tool that you and only you possess...

COACH: "...Your distinctly individual *creative imagination*."

While I agree that the *situation* is simply what's happening in the *conversation*, you can influence that element by creating a...

...Previously Occurring Incident (POI).

A **POI** exists in time before the beginning of the *conversation*, whether that be minutes, hours, days, weeks, months, or years before. The time frame is not important. What is important is that the **POI** pulls the trigger on the **SUB**-text of the Situation.

Here's what I mean.

The *Conversation*:

Two business associates meet in a café to discuss financial matters. One, a woman, is a client and the other, a man, is her financial broker. And that's the *situation*. Pretty straight-forward.

COACH (grins, winks): "Until you create the **POI**."

> **POI:** A ***Previously Occurring Incident*** is something that happened (in your imagination) before the beginning of the *conversation* that logically sets up your **SUB**-textural *need to be satisfied* through the other *character*.

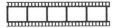

POI

The client had custody of her 9-year-old daughter today, and instead of hiring a babysitter after school, decided to bring her with her to the meeting. The client's been down on her luck recently and couldn't afford a babysitter. This is also why she is meeting with her broker, to see where she might free up some cash.

One block before they reach the café, they are crossing a dark alleyway when a homeless druggie jumps out of the shadows, grabs the girl, puts a knife to her throat, and tells the client to give him all her money or he'll kill her little girl. The client rips open her purse, pulls out her wallet, and opens it to show the druggie three dollar bills. Remember, she's broke and on her way to meet her finance guy.

COACH: "You created this as part of your **POI**."

The druggie furiously tells the client she has fifteen minutes to bring him $500 or he will kill her daughter, and if she tells anyone what is happening, he will kill the girl. As he drags the young, frightened girl back into the shadows, he repeats, "15 minutes or she's dead."

The Conversation begins in the café with the client sitting down at the table with her broker.

COACH: "Your **POI** is solidly in place."

So, do you think that **POI** will naturally, automatically generate **SUB**-text for that *situation*? Especially when, being the actor, you have read the script and you know that the broker tells you, the client, that he has fallen on bad times himself, is shutting down his business, and was hoping that you might be able to loan him a few bucks to put gas in his car.

ACTOR: "YIKES!"

Now, what do you think of the *situation*? Black and white? Not by a long shot. And it's all because of the **POI** you created with your *imagination*.

Now, I am not suggesting that was the right, or even the most appropriate **POI** to create and use, only that you have the option and the ability to provide yourself with information that is not on the page which can and will influence the situation as written.

COACH: "And Yes, again...**MYR**."

You can be as creative, as dangerous, as hilarious, as sad, as overjoyed as risky, or as safe as you choose to be in your creation of the **POI**. Although I always counsel against 'safe' or 'comfortable', as these are choices that can easily translate into 'boring'.

COACH: "And a bored audience means no audience at all."

I would only caution you to **Make Choices** that are aligned with the 'emotional content' of the scene...meaning, you would probably not Choose a **POI** that was hilarious if the *conversation* was taking place at a funeral. But, if you're up for taking a risk, maybe you would. Certainly make choices that interest you, that have you be interested, and that are tasty.

Just know that the only thing you cannot change, add to, or subtract from, are the **words** on the page. They are **written in stone** unless the director gives you the freedom to massage or change them. But, everything else is mutable.

And when the *relationship* is acted upon by a tasty **POI**, watch out, because sparks are sure to fly. **WOO-HOO!**

COACH: "The **POI** is part of your *preparation*, meaning you do not need to recall and or replay the details of the incident while you are actually having the conversation."

It's there, in the *preparation*, and will act upon you, emotionally and physically. It is your secret. No one else needs to know.

POINT FOUR: What's The TIME & PLACE?

Seemingly straightforward. Mostly overlooked... Extremely important.

Remember, you act best from your gut and your heart, not your brain, meaning, how 'you', the *character feel* about things, not what you, the actor *think* about things. And 'time and place' have a direct impact on how you *feel*.

COACH: "Think about it... as the *actor*, not the *character*."

Do you feel differently, physically and emotionally, at 3 a.m. than you do at 3 o'clock in the afternoon? And do you feel differently sitting on the beach on a stormy afternoon than you do sitting at a table in a very upscale restaurant? My guess is you're going to say: "Duh."

Well, the script will not always provide you with these little details, given that your *conversation* is typically 2-3 pages out of what is most often a 100-plus page screenplay. It's just not important info to include? Right?

COACH: "Given that none of us lives in a physical vacuum... *Wrong*!"

Two important ways Human beings relate to the world and those around us are through time and physical space. Given that the *characters* you're going to be asked to play are also human beings...

COACH *(grins)*: "Mostly."

...having these things in place is essential. So, if they are not defined in the conversation, then **Make** your own **Choices** about these two elements, and **Make Choices** that support the emotional content of the *conversation*. This will add internal layers to your *character*, generating, again, life behind the eyes. And remember to make them *tasty* **Choices**.

Here again, this becomes part of your *preparation*, not something You need to focus your attention on during the *conversation*. This information can be your secret as well if you *choose*, or you can *choose* to share this with the other *actor* in the scene so you can both be on the same page...

COACH: "Or better yet, on the same planet...HA!"

POINT FIVE: What's The NEED TO BE SATISFIED?

THE **NUMBER ONE** MOST Important Point! And this is *Absolutely* your **SECRET!** Share this with no one.

COACH: "**MYR...MYR...MYR!**"

All of the previous *Choices* you have made (#'s 1-4) using your *creative imagination* are in place basically to assist in the creation of, and to serve, this one **Ultimate *Choice***, the **NEED TO BE SATISFIED**. This is the **CHOICE** I am speaking about with the book's title, **MAKING CHOICES**. Without this **CHOICE** *Clearly*, *Simply,* and *Specifically* defined and in place, you will truly be flying...

COACH: "...By the seat of your pants."

Others refer to the *Choice* as an intention, a purpose, motivation, or want, but there is a real distinction between a **NEED TO BE SATISFIED** and these and other like terms. A **NEED** will grab you by the throat and drive or push you forward in the *conversation* until it is satisfied. A want, motivation, purpose, or intention, if it does not get fulfilled, will most likely be replaced by another want, motivation, purpose, or intention. It's not essential.

COACH: "But, **NEEDS** are!"

How much of your attention would be focused on finding air, if all of a sudden, there wasn't any? 25%? 50%? **100%!**

COACH: "That's a **NEED**!"

How much of your attention would be focused on getting a new red 'Vette like the one that just passed you on the freeway going 90? 25%? 50%? 100%? I doubt it.

COACH: "That's a Want."

According to American psychologist, Abraham Maslow, there are 7 Basic Human *NEEDS*:

- Air

- Water

- Food

- Shelter

- Sleep

- Safety

- Clothing

There is a universe of variations around these basic *NEEDS*, but what does not vary is that they, or their derivatives, will *Drive you Forward* until they are satisfied.

And that's the Key phrase...

Drive you Forward!

If You are being **Driven Forward** to Satisfy a **NEED**, something that is *important to you*...air, for example...wouldn't you say that you would have your *attention focused* wherever you needed it to be *focused* to get that **NEED** Satisfied?

COACH: "Of course."

Especially when there is a **CONSEQUENCE** to not getting the **NEED** SATISFIED which you must be UNWILLING TO ACCEPT. In this case, air or else...

COACH *(ominous)*: "*Dum, Dee, Dum, Dum.*"

This **CONSEQUENCE** is also a product of your *creative imagination* and is the lynchpin, the true catalyst for having your **NEED** to be satisfied' be effective. The **CONSEQUENCE**, given that it is *onerous, abhorrent, unimaginable*, and *unacceptable*, is what **Drives You**, what **MOTIVATES** you to be actively involved in getting Your **NEED** SATISFIED. So much so, that your attention would be focused on nothing else but SATISFYING YOUR **NEED**.

Now, if your **NEED** gets satisfied through you, then it makes sense that you would focus your attention on your-**SELF**. Right? Which would truly be **SELF**-*defeating*, given that the ultimate target we are shooting for is to...Act with **NO FEAR**

*NO FEAR can only exist when there is no **SELF**-Consciousness when you are Not Focused on 'you'.*

So, given that you *do* have a **CHOICE** as to where your attention is going to be focused...

COACH: "**Remember Challenge Two.**"

> **TIP: Challenge Two** - Refer to the section titled *Challenge Two* in Chapter 4.

...the obvious place to **Choose** to get your **NEED** satisfied is going to be outside of your-**SELF**. It also makes sense, if you are going to **Choose** someplace outside of your-**SELF** to focus your attention, the most advantageous place in a *conversation*...

COACH: "...Would be the other Character."

But, as odd as this may sound, even with a **NEED** to be SAT-ISFIED and a **CONSEQUENCE** in place for not getting the **NEED** satisfied, which must be so onerous that you, the *character*, are *un*willing to accept it...

COACH: "You are never going to speak the **NEED** out loud. You will *NOT* find it written in the text."

ACTOR: " What?"

COACH: "The **NEED** to be SATISFIED will always be a **SUB**-**TEXTURAL** **NEED**, created by your very alive *creative imagination*."

ACTOR: "That's crazy! If it's so bloody important, *WHY* on earth wouldn't you just come right out and say it, *demand* that it be satisfied?"

HERE'S WHY...

Have you ever been involved in a *conversation* with anyone where you **NEED**ed something from them, something important? But, you just knew that if you were to come right out and ask them to satisfy that **NEED**, they were going to say NO. You just *knew* it.

So, instead of going for the throat, instead of asking or demanding of them directly to satisfy your *SPECIFIC* **NEED**, you had a *conversation* with them about something else, something related to your **NEED**, something close to your **NEED**. In fact, you might even say the *conversation* you were having with them was meant to set up, to create the opportunity, for just the right moment, to come forward and finally, directly, ask for or demand the satisfaction of your **NEED**. A moment when you felt certain your *NEED* would be satisfied. Or even better, have them step forward and offer, unbidden by you...

COACH: "At least in words.

...to Satisfy your *NEED*."

In fact, you might even say you were influencing, maneuvering, or manipulating the *conversation* in the direction you *NEEDED* it to go to create just that right moment, the perfect opportunity to demand the satisfaction of your *SUB-TEXTURAL NEED*. Because your *NEED* was *so* important that you could not take a chance of *NOT* getting it satisfied.

And if all that was really true, then do you think you would be *paying* **Attention** to how the other person was behaving in the *conversation*, how they were responding and reacting to your manipulations, how they were *BEING* in every moment of that conversation? Their body language, the tone of the words coming out of their mouth, the way they paused at a particular moment, the way they looked away.

Would you not, in fact, become a **BIG EAR** that picks up all of the manifestations of their *communication* with you, just to be sure you didn't miss that opportunity, maybe the one and only opportunity you would ever have to get your *NEED* SATISFIED?

COACH: "*YES!* Definitely."

And during that *conversation*, do you think you would be spending much of your time *paying attention* to your-**SELF**, thinking about your-**SELF**, spending much of your time being **SELF**-Conscious? When, by thinking about your-**SELF**, by *paying* **attention** to your-**SELF**, you might miss that one opportunity to get your **NEED** SATISFIED through the other person?

And *should* you miss that one opportunity to get your **NEED** SATISFIED, you would absolutely be inviting the **CONSEQUENCE** which is **UNACCEPTABLE**, a *CONSEQUENCE* you would do anything to avoid? Is that something you would intentionally invite?

COACH: "Definitely, **NO!** And that's the way it happens in life. It's also, fortunately, the way it happens in acting, because, remember... *Acting is just like life.*"

THIS LEADS US TO...

Chapter Eight

The Crux Of The Matter

...IF THE PURPOSE OF the *work* is to have 'you' act with *NO FEAR*, and *NO FEAR* comes from a lack of *SELF*-Consciousness...

...*And,* you, the *actor,* have created a *SUB-TEXTURAL NEED TO BE SATISFIED* by you, the *character,* through the other *character* ONLY...

...*And,* if this *NEED* does not get SATISFIED, there is going to be a *CONSEQUENCE* to you, the *character,* which is UNACCEPTABLE...

...*Then,* WHERE is your *attention,* the *character's attention,* naturally going to be *focused*?

ACTOR: "On the *Other* Character...Right?"

And, you have become this **BIG EAR** that is *listening for,* and trying to make sense out of, all the *SUB*-Textural *conversation*...

COACH: "...Body language, tone of voice, ticks, behaviorisms, and on and on. Because that's where the real *conversation* is occurring."

Then, don't you think your mind, the *character's* mind, would be churning and churning, trying to make sense out of all that *SUB*-Textural communication, trying to determine if you are getting closer to that moment when you can get your *NEED* Satisfied, *or...*

COACH: "...further away from it, meaning you are getting closer to the occurrence of that Unacceptable *CONSEQUENCE*!"

So, with your *attention* fully focused on the other *character*, with the wheels going round and round inside your head, what is going to occur, *naturally*, with no conscious effort on your, the *actor's* part, simply by listening to and by paying attention to the other *character*, are the thoughts you, the Character, are having, moment by moment, about...what is going on with the other *character* in relation to whether or not you, the *character*, *think* you are getting your *NEED* Satisfied.

COACH: "That's right...take a deep breath. Just chew on that for a minute. In fact, it's socially acceptable to swallow this mega-bite more than once."

Because, the *conversation*, the **real** *conversation*, is not happening out loud.

COACH: "Remember, it's in the **SUB**-Text."

You, the *character*, will need to continually put 2 and 2 together...

COACH: "Body language here, tone of voice there...

...to see what you *think* it *really* adds up to...

2 + 2 = **NEED** Being Satisfied **or** *Not* Being Satisfied."

And, this creates that most wonderful, that most sought-after quality... *Life Behind the Eyes*...that **INNER LIFE**, which the camera, the director, and the audience are always hungry for.

> **INNER LIFE:** Thoughts, played out across the *character's* eyes, as they relate to whether or not the *character* believes they are getting their **SUB**-Textural Need to Be Satisfied accomplished.

You see, the camera is an internal, objective medium, with no opinion of its own, which reads the *character's* thoughts, the *character's* soul, through their eyes. For that to be interesting, you, the *character*, must be having thoughts connected to your underlying **SUB**-text, your underlying **NEED** to be satisfied...meaning connected to the truth, the *character's* truth, which is occurring in that very moment.

Put two *actors* on the screen, side by side. One is connected to an INNER LIFE, the other is not. Which one captures your attention, and which one are you going to watch?

COACH: "Which one do you want, do you **NEED**, to be?"

Having become a **BIG EAR**, you are paying attention to all *communication*. And as you take in the *communication*, making sense out of it in relation to the Satisfaction of your **NEED**, you wind up...

LISTENING FROM YOUR NEED TO BE SATISFIED: Meaning paying attention to what the other *character* has said or done and how it relates to having your **NEED** Satisfied.

SPEAKING INTO THE OTHER CHARACTER'S LIS-TENING: Focusing your full attention on influencing or manipulating the other *character* always in the perceived direction of getting your **NEED** Satisfied.

Can you get the importance of the **NEED** to be focused outside of your-**SELF**, focused on the other *character*, in order to get your **NEED** SATISFIED? It allows you no time to be focused on your-**SELF**...to be **SELF**-Conscious.

COACH: "At least, up until the *moment* you **get** your **NEED** satisfied."

ACTOR: "You mean before the scene, or the Conversation, is over?"

The Coach nods.

ACTOR: "Then what?"

Here's The WHAT

If and when You **get** your **NEED** satisfied, The **NEED** to focus your attention on the other *character* disappears, and you are once again able to focus your attention on...**YOU**, the **Actor**!

ACTOR: "OOOOOPS!!"

Meaning...you, the *character*, have disappeared, and you, the *actor*, have stepped back in because you have once again become **SELF**-Conscious.

In your right, reality-driven mind, you *know* you are the *actor*, not *really* the *character*...you know you can't really lift that classic Chevy off the unfortunate weekend mechanic! OMG!...

FEAR rushes in, you no longer trust the moment...*and*, there's one less weekend mechanic on the planet.

But, the *actor* cannot just say to themselves,...

"I need to focus my attention on the other actor because that will have me be present, in the moment, and will have me act with **NO FEAR.***"*

ACTOR: "I can't?"

COACH: "You can't just THINK your way into the *character*, into **NO FEAR**. That's mechanical."

You *act organically*, truthfully only from your heart and your gut. For those two organs (if you will) to be engaged, the *actor's* brain must be disengaged, must have been replaced with the *character's* brain, and operating logically as such. If there is a moment when the *actor* must step in to supply their thinking to satisfy a moment for the *character*, that is a mechanistic moment that destroys the *character's* reality. The real world comes rushing in, the *character* becomes the *actor*, **SELF**-Consciousness rules the day, and **FEAR** takes over.

- You start to think about the lines

- You think about the way you look

- You think about how you learned to say that very dramatic phrase and then you pay attention to your-*SELF* when you say it to be sure you said it the way you practiced it, and then you judge how well you said it

- You catch a brief glimpse of the casting director out of the corner of your eye with a frown on her face (not good!)

- You try to play the emotion of the scene (the character's mad for the entire scene)

- You think, "*Oh God*, I really need this job!"

- ...and on and on.

Without a **NEED** to be SATISFIED through the other *character*, forcing you to focus your attention off of your-**SELF** and onto the other *character*, in order to avoid the *UN*-acceptable **CONSEQUENCE**, you will think about your-**SELF**, become **SELF**-Conscious, try to make the words, the scene work instead of allow the *conversation*, the moment, to happen...

COACH: "You, the *actor*, will begin to **ACT!**"

ACTOR: "Not good, huh?"

COACH: "No worries. There's an easy fix. You don't just cut it off at the pass...you take an entirely different route."

Remember you, the *actor*, read the *conversation* and **Make** the **Choices** for you, the *character*.

And, because you, the *actor*, have read the *conversation*...

COACH: "Also known as the scene."

ACTOR: "Right."

...you know what is going to happen. Meaning, the *actor* can make a **Choice** of a **NEED** to be SATISFIED for the *character* that it's clear to see, can *NOT*, and will *NOT* get Satisfied in the *conversation*. Because, nowhere in the *conversation*, in the **TEXT**, does the **CLEAR, SIMPLE,** and **SPECIFIC NEED** to be SATISFIED (**Chosen** or created by the Actor, on **Purpose**) ever get Satisfied!

And then you, the *actor*, after having committed the **TEXT** so thoroughly to memory, you truly do not have to think about it, step into you, the *character*, and with your full attention focused on the other *character*, dive headlong into the pursuit of the satisfaction of the **NEED** through the other *character*, knowing there is a **CONSEQUENCE** to not getting the **NEED** satisfied you are *UN*-willing to accept, *but*...

COACH: "...**Not** having a clue that the *NEED* you, the *actor*, have chosen for you, the *character*, will never get Satisfied."

ACTOR: "Weird, but I think I'm getting it."

And, because the **NEED** does NOT get satisfied anywhere in the *conversation*, in the **TEXT**, you, the *character*, will have your attention focused outside of your-**SELF**, on the other *character*, in the *NOW*, for the entire scene, because that's *where* and *when* you need to get your **NEED** satisfied.

In fact, with the **CLEAR**, **SIMPLE,** and **SPECIFIC NEED** to be SATISFIED in place, you, the *character*, will have your attention fully focused on the other *character* from the moment before the *conversation* begins...

COACH: "Remember the POI!"

...until the moment after the *conversation* ends...*Or*, at least until you hear..."*CUT!*"

THE "ABBY"

ACTOR: "The what?"

COACH: "The Abby. The 2nd to the last shot of the day on a film. This means we're getting close. Hang in there."

Without the kind of structure in place described in **The CRUX**...

...forcing the attention of the *actor* to be outer-directed, the person in the *conversation* will always and only be the **SELF**-Conscious *actor*, who will be stuck in a *scene* that has a beginning, middle, and end, never the *character* in a *conversation* that exists in the **NOW**! And because for the *actor* it is only a *scene*, the opportunity for discovery, for being surprised *'in the moment'*, disappears and is replaced by a predictable future, where the *actor* is simply saying words she/he already knows they are going to say.

COACH: "Imagine if you really did know what was coming next."

ACTOR: " In life or acting?"

COACH: "Same thing, remember?"

ACTOR: "Yeah."

He pauses to consider.

ACTOR: "Sounds pretty cool...but, I think things might get boring pretty fast."

COACH: "And that's what happens to an audience watching an actor who's just spitting out lines from a scene they've memorized."

The actor smiles and gives a nod of understanding.

Chapter Nine

A Twist

COACH: "So, here's a *Twist*. What happens if the **NEED** the *actor* has chosen for themselves, for the *character*, is not working out?

ACTOR: "Whaddya mean?"

COACH: "The **TEXT** doesn't fit with the **SUB**-text. Meaning, how do you say *this*, the Text, when what you really mean is *that*, the **SUB**-text?"

ACTOR: "You mean, I can't get hung up on thinking I've got to say the words in a particular way."

COACH: "That's close. What I'm saying is that the words that are written on the page, the text, have no meaning on their own. They get their meaning or are informed only by your **SUB**-text."

ACTOR *(a little uncertain)*: "Uh hunh..."

COACH: "Ok, here's your third challenge."

Challenge THREE

Find a friend or a loved one, or at least someone who accepts your abnormal desire to be an *actor* (HA!). Look them right in the eyes and tell them...

ACTOR: "I love you."

...and mean it.

Ok, now get over the momentary flushed face and giggles, look them in the eyes again, and tell them...

ACTOR: "I hate you."

...and mean it. Yes, *really* mean it. You're an *actor*, remember?

Now once more, look them in the eyes and tell them, "I hate you", but this time, mean *"I Love you"*. Really mean it.

ACTOR *(sweetly)*: "I hate you."

A bit odd, I know.

Now once more. This time tell them, "I love you", but mean *"I hate you"*. Really.

ACTOR *(venomous)*: "I love you."

COACH: "Well?"

ACTOR: "Weird...but, interesting."

COACH: " Can you see that it doesn't matter what the **TEXT** says? What matters is Your **SUB**-text."

As long as you have ***Chosen*** a **Clear, Simple,** and **Specific** **SUB**-textural **NEED TO BE SATISFIED** through the other *character*, the **TEXT** will take care of itself.

ACTOR: "Yes, I can see that now."

COACH: "Good. So how about this?"

OBSTACLES

The ***NEED*** just seems too difficult to satisfy, for whatever reason. So, you decide to drop it, and pick up a new ***NEED*** midway through the *scene*. A ***NEED*** you, the *actor*, *think* will be easier...better.

Consider This:

You're a parent, and you're out walking with your 5-year-old. A nasty-looking guy comes riding by on a motorcycle and grabs your kid and rides off with the screaming toddler, laughing a loud, evil laugh as he clutches the youngster.

You yell, "*NO-O-O-O!!!*", and immediately give chase.

You race after the evil biker for 1 block, 2 blocks, 3 blocks...but you're losing ground and are almost out of energy.

The parent stops, out of breath.

PARENT *(disappointed, considers)*: "Heck, I'm never going to catch him."

The parent turns and walks into a café. Orders an iced cappuccino.

NO! That's *NEVER* going to Happen!

You would *NEVER* give up on your kid because you couldn't keep up with the kidnapper. You would find whatever other mode of transportation was available, like the cop's horse standing patiently by the cop while he is making time with the cute Uber driver. You'd leap into the saddle, grab the reins, and off you'd go in hot pursuit once again.

And if that didn't work, you'd try something else, and then something else, and then something else, until either you had rescued your kid or died trying because that's what parents do...

...*and* because the **CONSEQUENCE** of losing your child in that way, or any way actually, is unfathomable, unacceptable. You would *NEVER* give up.

COACH: "And that's how it is, how it has to be, with a **NEED** You have **Chosen** to be satisfied through the other *character*. When it becomes challenging to satisfy your **NEED**, You can't just give up and go grab an iced cappuccino."

The challenge simply means there is an **Obstacle** in your way that you must deal with, which you must overcome, get over, around, or through to Satisfy your **NEED**. Because, if you don't, then the **CONSEQUENCE** will certainly occur. And if it's a **CONSEQUENCE** you are unwilling to accept, you will either succeed in overcoming it or die trying.

COACH *(to the Actor)*: "You get the idea?"

The Actor nods.

You also **NEED** to get that having an **Obstacle** to overcome is a *good* thing. In fact, you will find that you, the *actor*, will eventually create **NEEDS** to be satisfied that have obstacles built in for you, the *character*, because they require you to become more *involved*, more focused outside of your-**SELF**, more *'alive in the moment'*, more Present in the process of overcoming them.

OBSTACLE: Anything that stands in the way of you achieving your **NEED TO BE SATISFIED**. Can be **External, Internal**, or both.

There are two kinds of ***OBSTACLES*** to consider:

External

The evil biker is clearly an external obstacle... something that is a product of the outside world that you will ***NEED*** to deal with, to overcome.

Internal

An internal obstacle could be your desperate addiction to iced cappuccinos which you will have to struggle against in order to save your child.

ACTOR: "**HA!**..."

COACH: "Yes, that's stretching it just a bit."

A better example, not associated with the evil biker scenario, would be if you, the *character*, **NEED**ed your ex-lover to tell you they still loved you, or else you were going to end it all. The harder you tried to get your ***NEED*** satisfied, the more desperate and upset you became, and the more reluctant your ex was becoming to say *anything* nice to you.

For you to overcome this Internal obstacle (your anger and frustration), you must first become aware of your anger, realize it is a problem, and in the moment, calm your-**SELF**, look for a way to repair the damage you have done, and do whatever is necessary to get your **NEED** Satisfied.

COACH: "Or else..."

And consider what this does for you, the *character*, regarding the creation of *life behind the eyes*, the *Inner Life*. Thinking on the fly about how to overcome an internal obstacle will have those inner wheels turning and burning. And it will all be directly related to your **SUB**-Textural **Choice**. The casting director, the director, the audience, and the camera will eat it up.

COACH: "So, given that there are **NO** absolutes in this world or any others, here's the **EXCEPTION TO THE RULE** of **NEVER** giving up on the **NEED** you have **Chosen** to be Satisfied.

ACTOR: "AHA! I knew it!"

COACH: "And you just happen to be even more right than you think you are."

ACTOR: "I am?"

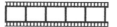

The AHA Moment

Let's go back to the evil biker and the kidnapped kid scenario.

EXT. CITY STREET - DAY

You're galloping down the street as fast as the horse can go, maybe faster. You're actually closing the gap.

PARENT *(to the horse)*: "Go horse, GO!"

The evil biker turns back for another look and lets out another evil burst of laughter. He turns back just in time to see the cars in front of him have come to a dead stop, but not in time to swerve to avoid them.

The biker slams on the brakes, smoke pours from the burning rubber of his tires.

You watch in horror as the bike slams into the car directly in front of him.

PARENT: "JOHNNY!!!!!!!!"

Both the biker and the boy go flying, the biker smashing into the car, and Johnny onto a grassy section on the side of the road. You gallop up to the grassy section, leap off the trigger, and rush to little Johnny's side. He's out cold, but he's still breathing.

PARENT: "Thank the Lord..."

You look up frantically at the crowd gathering around you.

PARENT: "Are any of you a doctor?"

No response.

BYSTANDER 1: "There's a hospital 4 blocks down the street."

AHA! A Hospital!

You gather little Johnny up into your arms, rush to the street, where you yank the little old lady out of her '72 Chevy Nova, place Johnny on the seat next to you, then lay rubber as you speed off down the street towards the hospital.

COACH *(to the Actor)*: "Can you guess what the exception to the rule is of **NEVER** giving up on the **_NEED_** you have ***Chosen*** to be Satisfied?

ACTOR: "Aha?"

COACH: "Right you are. The '***AHA MOMENT***'. And can you guess what that is?"

ACTOR: "Ummm...?"

A **TRANSITION,** from one **NEED** to be satisfied to a new **NEED** to be satisfied in the same *conversation*. And while the little Johnny *conversation...*

COACH: "Aka the scene."

...is a long *conversation*, but it is still the same *conversation*.

To be clear, the little Johnny *conversation* is written in an extremely blatant fashion to make the point. The **NEEDS** to be satisfied are so obvious that you would have to say they are in no way **SUB**-Textural:

> 1. to the Evil Biker: I **NEED** you to STOP!

> 2. to little Johnny: I **NEED** you to keep breathing.

ACTOR: "So, what's... **The POINT?**"

If the first **NEED** to be satisfied gets satisfied before the *conversation* has ended, there must be a *transition* to a new **NEED** to be satisfied that takes you to the end of the *conversation*, and actually into the moment after the *conversation* has ended, or at least until you, the *actor*, hears "**CUT!**"

Because, as long as you, the *character*, has a **NEED** to be satisfied outside of your-**SELF**, that's where your attention will be focused, meaning you cannot be conscious of your-**SELF**, the *actor*, meaning you will be *present in the moment*, and You will experience **NO FEAR.**

Chapter Ten

Right Or Wrong

ACTOR: "I've got a question. Been bothering me about this whole **Making Choices** approach."

COACH: "Ok. Let's hear it."

ACTOR: "How do you know what the **Right Choice** is, and how do you avoid the **Wrong Choice**?"

COACH: "AHA!"

There are **NO** Right **Choices** and there are **NO** Wrong **Choices**. There is a universe of *possible* **Choices**, some of which will prove much *tastier* than others. You try one on to see if and how it fits your *conversation*. If it's not a good fit, discard it and try another.

COACH: "But,... No matter how uncomfortable or wrong the **NEED** you have **Chosen** may seem during the course of your *conversation,* you stick with that **NEED** to be satisfied through the other *character* until you hear **"CUT!"**

You might just find out that as wrong as your **Choice** may have at first seemed, it actually created the kind of **Obstacles** and the kind of odd and interesting **SUB**-text that landed you the callback, maybe even the job.

Even with the understanding that there is a universe of *possible* **Choices**, *actors*, in the heat of the moment, will historically, and hysterically, have trouble coming up with any **SUB**-textural **Choices**.

COACH: "Like swallowing too much ice cream in one gulp, brain freeze sets in. You can't come up with even one...out of a possible universe of **Choices**."

ACTOR: "So, what's the answer?"

COACH: "The bottom line, of course."

ACTOR: "Meaning?"

COACH: "The *only* Wrong **Choice** you can **Make**, is not to **Make** *any* **Choice** at all!"

ACTOR *(frustrated)*: "Great."

COACH: "But, there is a shortcut."

ACTOR *(brightens)*: "Really?"

COACH: "Yep. Keep reading."

The "I NEED YOU TO..." Cheat Sheet

Ok, you've got a big audition for that once-in-a-lifetime role. You're the prosecuting attorney cross-examining the lead in the film, for murder. If you get this role, you just know it's going to open the floodgates for more quality work to come. It's a killer *conversation*, and it's a self-taped audition. So, your **Choice** of a **NEED** to be satisfied has got to be a killer **Choice** too. No pressure, right?

What to do?... What to do?

COACH: "You pull out your **'I NEED YOU TO...'** Cheat Sheet. Go down your list of ten 'I **NEED** YOU TO...' **Choices** and, *voila*, you land on the one **Choice** that is really tasty: #7"

"I NEED YOU TO..." Cheat Sheet Example

    1. I need you to...xxxxxxx

    2.

I need you to...xxxxxxx

3. I need you to...xxxxxxx

4. I need you to...xxxxxxx

5. I need you to...xxxxxxx

6. I need you to...xxxxxxx

7. I need you to...***Lose your temper!***

8. I need you to...xxxxxxx

9. I need you to...xxxxxxx

10. I need you to...xxxxxxx

That's the one that does it for you, the one that has you in action, that you can see would satisfy your **NEED**. And it doesn't matter that you've used it numerous times before because you will behave differently with each new *character*, each new *relationship*, each new *situation*, each new *take*, and on and on. The **NEED** can remain the same, but everything else changes.

Even with the same *conversation*, the same *characters*, and the exact same words, everything changes, because it *Must*. Because time moves on relentlessly. Nothing can ever be repeated. Nothing remains the same. Except for the words on the page that You have memorized and your **Choice** of the **NEED** TO BE SAT-ISFIED. This allows you, the *actor*, to come as close as possible to *repeat* the magic of that last take that the director absolutely *loved*, but cannot use because there was a major problem with the sound.

No worries. Stick with *Lucky #7*, and your next take will be as close to a repeat as is humanly possible. And, you are not think-ing as the *actor*, trying to duplicate what you just did. Instead, you are *alive in the present moment*, as the *character*, in action, pursuing a **NEED** to be satisfied through the other *character*, meaning your attention will be focused outside of your-**SELF**, so you will not be **SELF**-Conscious, allowing you to experience that most blissful of states...

...NO FEAR.

COACH: "AND NOW IT's your turn."

ACTOR: "My turn?"

COACH: "Yes. Make your List."

ACTOR: "Work, work, work..."

COACH: "Don't you love it?"

ACTOR: "Yes...I really do...HA!"

Your "I NEED YOU TO..." Cheat Sheet

I need you to...	
I need you to...	
I need you to...	
I need you to...	
I need you to...	
I need you to...	
I need you to...	
I need you to...	

ACTOR: " **OMG!**... There's so much to think about! What happened to **CLEAR**, **SIMPLE,** and **SPECIFIC**?!"

COACH: " Hang in there. It's coming. But, I like your sense of *urgency*. And speaking of..."

POINT SIX: What Is The URGENCY?

URGENCY is created by something happening at a *time certain*...

COACH: "Pivotal word."

...in the Future, and the sooner in the future, the greater the **URGENCY**.

What **URGENCY** is not intended to have you, the *character*, do is speak faster. That may occur *naturally*, but that is definitely not the purpose of **URGENCY**.

ACTOR: "So? What difference does **URGENCY** make to me in a *Conversation*?"

COACH: "Consider this..."

Would you be more committed to, more involved with, and more focused on getting your **NEED** satisfied in the *conversation* you are having right now if:

　　1. You had two weeks to get it satisfied, or...

　　2. Right **NOW** is the only chance you are **ever** going to have to get it satisfied?

COACH: "I am guessing # 2 is your answer."

ACTOR *(nods)*: "Yep."

And, given that to get your **NEED** satisfied, you must keep your attention focused on the other *character* in the conversation, might this sense of **URGENCY** help? Especially if by staying focused and getting your *NEED* satisfied, you are avoiding an *un*acceptable *CONSEQUENCE?*

And remember, there is the *actor* and there is the *character*, who are both the same person, **You**, but never both at the same time. The *actor* makes the choices for the *character*, and the *character* lives out those Choices.

Also, the *actor* knows the *character* is doing a scene, with a beginning, middle, and end, and would therefore say that they need to get their *NEED* TO BE SATISFIED accomplished by the end of the *scene, but...*

COACH: "...The Character, just like you in your life, is involved in a *conversation* where they must get that *NEED* SATISFIED **NOW**...

...And if it does NOT get Satisfied **NOW**, then it *Really Needs* to get satisfied *NOW!*...and every moment it does *NOT* get satisfied, it becomes that much *more* **URGENT** to get it satisfied...

...Especially if this is going to be your one and only chance to get it satisfied."

And the more **URGENCY** that is created, the more actively involved you, the *character*, becomes in pursuing the satisfaction of your *NEED*, because the closer you are getting to that looming *CONSEQUENCE*.

COACH: "So, given these dynamics created and generated by **URGENCY**, how much of your time, the *character's* time, do you think you will spend thinking about Your-**SELF**...the Actor's **SELF**?"

ACTOR: " How about none?"

COACH *(smiles)*: "Good guess. And now, back to your earlier **URGENT** question..."

ACTOR: "***OMG!*...** *There's so much to think about! What happened to **CLEAR, SIMPLE,** and **SPECIFIC**?!*"

Chapter Eleven

Fine Point "Finale"

COACH: "Well, congrats! You've made it this far, and here comes your reward."

Out of all the points which have been hit upon or discussed in this guide, there is really only **_ONE point_** that you, the *character*, **_NEED_** to recall, remind yourself of, and think about.

COACH: "And I'd lay odds that you know what that **_ONE point_** is..."

ACTOR *(smiles)*: "I NEED YOU TO..."

The coach raises a thumb skyward.

COACH: "Bingo! But wait..."

ACTOR: "What Now?"

COACH: "I know you've got the **Handle** on ***MAKING CHOICES*** right now, but...just in case you ***NEED*** a quick reminder in the future, how about a..."

...Points Summary

I - POINT ONE: <u>*WHO* Are You?</u>

Meaning, ***who*** are you as the *character*? Know the *character* as well as you know your-***SELF***.

II - POINT TWO: <u>What's the RELATIONSHIP?</u>

Meaning the ***relationship*** between you and the other *character* or *characters* you are in conversation with.

What is the nature, quality, and dynamic of that *relationship* that creates the nuances of your *character*?

Don't forget to ***People*** your scene.

III - POINT THREE: <u>What's The *SITUATION*?</u>

Meaning literally, what's *happening* in the *conversation*?

Don't forget to create a *'tasty'* **POI (Previously Occurring Incident)**.

IV – POINT FOUR: <u>What's The *TIME* And *PLACE?*</u>

Seemingly straightforward. Mostly overlooked. Extremely important.

Remember, you act best from your gut and your heart, not your brain... meaning, how *you*, the character *feels* about things, not what you, the *actor*, *think* about things. And *time* and *place* have a direct impact on how you *feel*.

If these elements are not defined in the *conversation*, create them as they create nuance.

V - POINT FIVE: <u>What's The *NEED TO BE SATISFIED?*</u>

The ***NUMBER ONE*** most important point! And this is *absolutely* your SECRET! Share this with no one.

Use your imagination to create as challenging and as tasty a **NEED *TO BE* SATISFIED** as possible.

- It is definitely a NEED, not a Want.

- It is a SUB-Textural NEED, never spoken out loud.

- It gets Satisfied through the other *character* only.

- It always languaged as "I Need You To..."

- There is a logical urgency in place to get the NEED satisfied.

- There are obstacles to overcome in satisfying the NEED.

- There is a CONSEQUENCE to not getting the NEED satisfied which you must be unwilling to accept.

- It is a NEED that you, as the *actor*, cannot see gets satisfied in the *CONVERSATION*.

VI - POINT SIX: What Is The <u>URGENCY</u>?

URGENCY is created by something happening at a *time certain,* in the future, and the sooner in the future, the greater the **URGENCY**.

Whatever creates the **URGENCY** must be logical to the Character.

COACH: "EVERYTHING ELSE IS the Actor's..."

Chapter Twelve

Preparation

THIS IS PART OF your **Preparation**, meaning you do not need to recall and or replay the details while you are actually in the *conversation*. It's there, in the **Preparation**, and will act upon you, emotionally and physically...

It's like Loading your-**SELF** with all of the information and experience you'll ever need to drive a car. Once you are driving, you don't need to look at the driving manual or remind your-**SELF** of how the car works. You simply drive.

ACTOR: "So, it's all just preparation?"

COACH: "Where **Preparation** is concerned, there is no **"just"**."

Preparation is an absolute necessity for the life and **Choices** of the *character*. But, it needs to be put into its proper perspective. And the best way to do that is via an analogy.

COACH *(grins)*: "I love analogies."

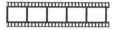

Preparation Analogy

Think back to the days of yore. And I mean *real* yore...like Gladiator yore.

COACH: "Or, if you'd prefer, think back to the day you saw the movie, **GLADIATOR**. Either one should do."

Gladiators were typically enslaved killers, fighters, who would enter an arena and fight for their life...to the death! Either against other gladiators or any number of varieties of hungry beasts.

COACH: "You lose, you're lunch."

The gladiators would be herded into a holding pen or cell, where they would anxiously await their turn to do battle. This time would be spent in **Preparation** for their upcoming fight. They would choose their weapon, practice their moves, they would warm up, pray to their god or gods, would scrutinize the other gladiators they either knew they would be fighting or be in deep thought and meditation visualizing their fight to come. They would think back on all of their practice in **Preparation** for this one day, this one fight. And depending on how well **Prepared** they were, that could mean the difference between victory and defeat.

Then the trumpets would blare, signaling the beginning of the 'games'. The gate to the arena would open. They would step out of the relative safety of the cell, singly or as a group, and their real struggle would begin. To the death. In real-time.

COACH: "Now imagine, you are one of those gladiators."

You have just been ushered into the fighting arena. You have a small sword in your sweaty hands. You look up, and here comes the monster of a man you had been watching in the holding cell, the one you prayed would be dispatched before he even knew you were there. He carries a huge axe which he effortlessly tosses back and forth between his bear-like hands.

COACH: "He has murder in his eyes, spittle dripping from his maw of a mouth...and he's headed straight for you."

"OMG!", you think. *"Should I jab my sword at his ankle, as I practiced, or maybe an uppercut to his thigh? I've seen that work before. And did I spend enough time praying this morning, and visualizing a successful outcome...?"*

COACH: "The monster's on top of you, and here comes the *AXE...*"

ACTOR *(dripping* *sweat)*: **"RUN-N-N-N-N-N-N-N-N-N!!!!!!!"**

COACH: "Exactly. The bottom line is if you are still thinking about or in the middle of **Preparation** when it comes time to be in **ACTION**...off with his head!

When you hear **ACTION** (or some facsimile), you *Trust* the **Preparation** you have already done, and you live in the moment...with only **One Thought** in mind..."

ACTOR: "I Need You To..."

COACH *(smiles, nods)*: "In the case of our monster gladiator, it might be, I Need You To...

ACTOR: "**...Fall on your Axe!**"

COACH: "Good **Choice.**"

From that moment on, your only thoughts and actions are going to be focused on how to have that happen, until the moment the monster is a goner! And you will consciously and unconsciously call upon all of your **Preparation**, in real-time, to have that happen. Because all of your actions will be in direct relation to the **Preparation** you have done around Who you are, the *relationship*, the *situation*, *time* and *place*, and *urgency*.

And they are all in place for the one purpose of you avoiding the **CONSEQUENCE** of you not getting Your **NEED** satisfied...

ACTOR: "**Death** by a spittle drooling, monster gladiator!"

COACH *(grins)*: "Or something like it."

For those of you visually oriented...

COACH: "Most of you, I would guess."

...You can think of your **Preparation** as a *funnel*.

You dump all of the aspects of **Preparation**, including the dynamics and nuance of each, into the top of the funnel. They all filter down to **One CLEAR, SIMPLE,** and **SPECIFIC** Point...

ACTOR: "The **NEED TO BE SATISFIED...**"

COACH: "...Through the Other *character!*"

You TRUST that, and it will **Drive You Forward**, in *action, alive* and *present, in the moment,* with NO **SELF**-CONSCIOUSNESS.

COACH: "And the best part of all...with...?"

ACTOR *(smiles)*: "*...NO FEAR!*"

Chapter Thirteen

It's Almost A Wrap!

COACH: "Oh no, no, NO! You can't go quite yet! Did you hear "*CUT*"?...Didn't think so."

We haven't gotten our **NEED Satisfied** with you yet! We **NEED** you to take this little quiz, or else...

COACH: "...My goldfish is going to go into a deep depression, and drown. And I am going to feel totally responsible and guilty for that preventable tragedy, which I absolutely *KNOW* I will not be able to live with, boo hoo...

...HA!

Have Fun!

Chapter Fourteen

Fun Work

Quiz Scene

INT. HOSPITAL ROOM – NIGHT

A worn and exhausted, obviously frail elderly man/woman, ALBERT/ALICE, lies in the partially raised hospital bed. The antiseptic hospital sheet barely rises and falls with the man's/woman's shallow breathing. His/Her eyes are closed, actively dreaming as evidenced by the movement beneath the lids.

The sound of the door opening causes his/her eyelids to flutter, and slowly open. His/Her blurred vision comes into focus on the middle-aged woman/man, TERRY/THOMAS, as she/he steps up to the side of the bed. The trench coat she's/he's wearing and her/his hair is soaked. She/He reaches for the frail hand, but the old man/woman pulls it away. Terry/Thomas tries to brush it off.

TERRY/THOMAS: "Hey Pop. How ya doing?"

ALBERT/ALICE: "Just peachy. You?"

Terry/Thomas removes her/his dripping coat and pulls an envelope out of the pocket.

TERRY/THOMAS *(grins)*: "Cold and wet. Got a real nor'easter blowin' out there."

ALBERT/ALICE *(suspicious)*: "What are you doing here, Terry/Thomas?"

She/He hesitates.

TERRY/THOMAS: "I...I've got to take an earlier flight tomorrow, in the morning. They're canceling everything afternoon because of the storm..."

ALBERT/ALICE: "And what? You might get stuck here, huh? Can't let that happen, can you?"

He/She cocks his/her head toward his uncomfortable daughter/son.

ALBERT/ALICE: "Haven't seen you in two years, and now you got to hurry up and leave. Guess I should've tried dyin' more often."

Can't stop himself/herself from a hoarse laugh, which turns into convulsive coughing. Terry/Thomas steps in to help.

TERRY/THOMAS: "Easy Dad/Mom, easy..."

She/He eases her/his father/mother back down to his/her pillow.

TERRY/THOMAS: "I'm sorry, Dad/Mom, but I've got a meeting..."

ALBERT/ALICE *(struggles)*: "Yeah, yeah, I know how important those big meetings are."

Terry/Thomas still holds the envelope in her/his hand, uncertain what to do, what to say next.

TERRY/THOMAS: "Dad/Mom...

They connect, both struggling for their next words. Finally,

ALBERT/ALICE: "Get out of here, ok. Got to get my beauty rest. I want to look good for my trip too, you know."

Terry/Thomas again, unsure what to say. She/He grabs her/his coat, folds the envelope in her/his hand, and puts it back in the pocket.

TERRY/THOMAS: "Sure."

She/He turns for the door.

ALBERT/ALICE: "Ter/Tom..."

She/He stops and turns back. Albert/Alice struggles for the right words.

ALBERT/ALICE: "Thanks...for comin'."

Terry/Thomas hesitates, nods, turns, and goes out the door.

Albert/Alice stares at the ceiling.

ALBERT/ALICE *(sighs)*: "Just great."

FADE TO BLACK.

OK. LET'S SEE WHAT you got from this guide.

Grab a piece of paper (I think my age just showed - HA!), or your device of choice, and take your time with the Quiz below. Take it often to sharpen your skills. Remember, it's not possible to fail.

Learn and grow as an *artist* and a *craftsperson*. Oh yeah... and as a human *being*!

PRICE & COACH & ACTOR...

And don't forget...**MYR!** Do it for You.

Quiz

<u>WHO</u> are you as the *character*? (*CHOOSE* ONE from the above conversation)

Be detailed about the *character's* life.

- Write it down by hand.

What's the <u>RELATIONSHIP</u> between you, as the *character*, and the other *character*?

- **<u>PEOPLE</u> the *relationship*.**

    - Who in your life is this person to you, that makes you FEEL the way the other *character* makes you, the *character*, FEEL?

    - What is the DYNAMIC of the Relationship?

        - Do you have a His/Her story with the other *character* that colors the *relationship*?

What's the <u>SITUATION</u>?

At face value, it's what's going on in the *conversation*, what's written in black and white.

- What's the DYMANIC of the *situation*?

  - What's the *Previously Occurring Incident* (**POI**) that informs or incites or pulls the trigger on the *situation*?

What are the <u>TIME</u> and <u>PLACE</u>?

1. They may be provided in black and white, but if not, create them.

Take some time to create the PLACE (the physical reality... visualize it) and the FEELING of the TIME

What's your *<u>NEED TO BE SATISFIED</u>*?

Only gets SATISFIED through the other *character(s)*.

- You language it to yourself as: I NEED you to..., instead of simply I Need...

- Keep the NEED Clear, Simple & Specific. You don't need to complicate the NEED, as you, the human being, are already complicated enough.

- It is a SUB-TEXTURAL *NEED* (never gets expressed in the dialogue).

- It *DOES NOT* get SATISFIED in the *conversation*.

- There is a **CONSEQUENCE** to not getting the **NEED** satisfied which the *character* must be *UN*-Willing to accept. What is your **CONSEQUENCE**?

What's the <u>URGENCY</u>?

Urgency is created by something occurring at a time CERTAIN in the Future.

- What has this been the only time that you will ever be able to get your *NEED* SATISFIED, and WHY?

1. What are the **OBSTACLES**, internal or external, to getting the *NEED* SATISFIED?

2. WHAT ARE YOU WAITING FOR? TIME'S A FLYING! GO GET YOUR *NEED* SATISFIED, AL-READY! *HA!*

CONGRATS!!

That's a CUT...

That's a Wrap!

Chapter Fifteen

Final Note

A BRILLIANT ACTING TEACHER of mine once said that Actors are like magicians who walk around with a bag of tricks, deciding which of those tricks to pull out and use at any given moment. The *actor* must know how to make use of those tricks, and to do that they must know how and why they work.

I've just given you my big trick as well as the what, how, and why. I trust you will add to it, expand it, claim it as your own, own it as your *way*, make excellent use of it, and have an amazing experience and a great life in the process.

However, or why-ever, you have found your way to this page, I want you to know that no matter where you are along your path to exploring or fulfilling your desires to *act*, or simply to live your life in the present, I am already your biggest fan.

By reading this far, you've proven you have the desire to learn and grow as an Actor, as an artist, and as a *Human Being*. Now all that's required is for you to take that next step. And then keep *following through*. The **NO FEAR** part will show up when you least expect it, and guess what...when it does, it will infect your entire life. So, if you stay with it, and even if you don't, once you have started down this road, your life will never be the same.

It will be better.

Afterword by Mary Jo Slater

As a casting director, I have witnessed firsthand the incredible power of an actor's creative character development. With this book, MAKING CHOICES for the Successful Actor: The Actor's Preparation Guide to Creative Character Development, you have the tools to take your performance to the next level.

This book is an essential resource for any actor looking to create powerful performances. From understanding the essential elements of character building to the practical exercises for exploring characters, this book will help you realize your potential as an actor.

I highly recommend this book for any actor seeking to develop their craft and make their mark on the industry. Congratulations on a job well done!

Mary Jo Slater

Casting Director

Dedication

There have been numerous people along the way who have taught me, gotten me excited about, and instilled deeply in me the passion, love, and commitment to the Craft of Acting. Those that stand out in my mind were: Jeff Corey, Dennis Moore, John Lehne, and Vincent Chase. Each, in their own particular way, did something to me and stimulated me in some profound way, not simply as an actor, but as a human being. They evoked in me a broader sense of Being Here Now that has stayed with me and influenced the way I experience my own unique world. They helped me come to trust that the world I experience is the world that matters, and in trusting that, if I can just allow that world to be expressed through my Craft, I might find that common ground where all humanity agrees, through the heart, not the brain. I am thankful for the insight and understanding they bestowed upon me.

I am also deeply indebted to an old friend and colleague who probably does not recall the gift he bestowed upon me...the gift of teaching, which I believe I may cherish even more than I do the primary experience of Acting, blasphemous as that may sound.

When I was in the midst of the pursuit of my own professional acting career some years back (how many years will remain my secret – LOL!), a resident of Venice Beach in LA, I received a phone call one afternoon from this old friend. He told me that he had been teaching an improv class at a modeling and talent agency in Costa Mesa, CA, south of LA by about 45 minutes (3 hours at rush hour – No kidding) in Orange County.

He said they were offering opportunities for new teachers to come down and test out their teaching skills on their clients, and that he thought I might be good teaching material. Would I like to have a shot at teaching one class on any aspect of the craft that interested me? The first thought that came to my mind produced a loud, nervous laugh, immediately followed by me, driven by some itch that existed deep within, saying, "Yes". That was immediately followed by a silent, internal shout, "WHAT, ARE YOU OUT OF YOUR MIND?!" But, it was too late. I was hooked and booked.

I spent three weeks preparing for that one class, reading book upon book about the Craft, going over my own notes taken in my own acting classes, making new notes upon notes on a pile of 3 x 5 index cards, trying to prepare myself for what I assumed would be my first and my last teaching gig.

The night arrived, and the room was standing room only, filled with curious and excited actors who I was certain were there not so much to learn about the Craft of Acting, as they were anticipating a night of hilarious embarrassment of another fresh meat teaching hopeful. This included, of course, my friend who had arranged for the comedic carnage.

The owner of the agency stepped up to the front of the room, cool and calm, and introduced me. I think the students were applauding as I made my way to the makeshift podium, but I still can't be sure from the sound of the incessant and loud beat of my heart throbbing in my ears. But, I am extremely clear about what happened from that moment forward.

I reached into my coat pocket, dragged out the now-worn pile of index cards with all of my hand-scrawled notes, took one final look at my opening lines, and started reading before I had even looked up. And then I did, and then it happened.

The connection.

With the students, and the people in the room. They were looking at me, and for the first time, I was really looking at them. I
stopped reading and took a deep breath, the room was silent. I
looked to the back of the room and saw my good friend, smiling
and nodding his enthusiastic support...his name is Jed Mills, by
the way, a brilliant actor and teacher in his own right, and still,
years later, a dear friend.

In those few moments, I connected with what I would later
come to realize was, and call, the rhythm of life, which, like a
wheel, goes round and round continually. If you miss the jumping in place on this revolution, don't worry, it will come back
around again in its own time, allowing you the opportunity to
connect with that natural rhythm.

In the moments before jumping back in, I gently moved my note
cards from my hands back into my coat pocket, re-connected
with my audience, and opened my mouth. From that day to this,
the words have simply fallen from my mouth, without a note
card in site, and I have loved every minute of it.

Thank you, Jed.

Price Hall

The Natural Act

Invitation

ALL OF US HERE at *The Natural Act* trust you had a great experience reading this Guide and that it helped inspire you to keep putting one foot in front of the other because Acting is truly not about the destination. It is absolutely about the journey. May yours be enlivening!

Please send us your feedback on this Guide. We'd love to hear it. And feel free to keep us posted on your Acting career. We are interested.

With that in mind, please consider having me or one of my protégés come to your hometown to lead a 1 or a 2-day workshop on **MAKING CHOICES**. It will absolutely boost the level of your craft, as well as answer your questions about what to do going forward with your career.

We can also schedule private 1 on 1 sessions on acting for the camera with you, either face-to-face when we are there for workshops, or online at any time. We would love to help you in the growth of your *craft* and your professional career endeavors. We'd be happy to discuss the possibilities with you.

And if you've ever thought about, or had a desire, or not (like me...HA!), to try your hand at being an Acting Teacher or Coach (insert *Your Name* where the 'Coach' appears in this Guide), The Natural Act is now accepting applications for our ***MAKING CHOICES*** Coach Training Program, which will lead to becoming a Certified Natural Act Instructor. This is a hands-on, at-home training course in The Natural Act approach or a Way to train and coach Actors to become working professionals.

Feel free to write us, giving us a short description of WHO you are, what if any, experience you may or may not have had (not required) as an Actor and/or Acting Instructor, and Why you feel you would be an inspiring Instructor. We welcome you to apply. An application will be sent to you after your initial contact and expression of interest.

Remember, The Natural Act is Where Acting Comes Naturally.

Thank you for taking the journey of ***MAKING CHOICES*** with us. We hope to hear from you soon.

Price Hall | The Natural Act

thenaturalact2@gmail.com

www.thenaturalact.net

www.beherenownaturally.com

Special Thanks

SPECIAL THANKS TO MY wife, Juli, for her unswayed support in getting over, around, or through the inevitable obstacles of my own inner resistance in getting this *bloody* (Thank you, Malcolm!) book done, and my mother for her unbridled enthusiasm which infected me and defined my **NEED** to complete this Guide or suffer the *Consequence* of my own guilt for not being able to put the completed, physical book into her frail and loving hands...which I did on July 6th, 2018. She was giddy...HA!

And Special Mention to Terry Futschik, my trusty associate, and Chelsea Lee, for their enthusiastic and painstaking support in helping put this Work together.

And a Special, Special *THANK YOU* to the Angel who flew in at the finish line to truly make this Guide a *WRAP* - Thank you, Christin Tolentino!

Cheers to you all!

Price

About Price Hall

Price Hall is an entertainment industry veteran of 35-plus years. A premier acting teacher, legendary director, producer, and coach who is known for producing and directing Hollywood movies: Mississippi Murder, Dancing in Twilight, Swing Vote, and Being Rose.

Known as one of the most popular acting coaches from Houston, Texas to Hollywood, Hall's cutting-edge acting technique has helped famous actors such as Malcolm McDowell, Luke Goss, Bryan Batt, Kate Orsini, Hani Furstenberg, Thomas Francis Murphy, Christopher Emerson, Phillip Fornah, Jay Caputo, Jameshia Bankston, and Joe DeMonico to further their successful acting careers.

Price Hall has founded REPERTORY FILMS and THE NATURAL ACT to teach, coach, and direct actors and coaches in his approach to acting for the camera and MAKING CHOIC-ES, which leads to Acting Naturally.

Hall grew up in the idyllic small Virginia town of Bon Air, across the James River from Richmond. An adventurer from the beginning, his love of photography and exploration led him to visit and work on different continents, which has further expanded his exposure and experience. With over 35 years of experience in coaching actors, coaches, and real people, and directing movies, Price Hall wanted his techniques to reach a wider audience who are seeking to get more out of life by Being Naturally Present in every Moment as actors, coaches or simply as human beings. Hall has therefore released his latest book - MAKING CHOIC-ES for the SUCCESSFUL ACTOR: The Actor's Preparation Guide to Creative Character Development.

Because Price believes deeply that all good acting is just like Life, he recommends his book to anyone truly interested in a conversation about an approach to Being Alive & Present every moment of their Lives. It is simply about Making A Choice.

Price is a graduate of Hampden-Sydney College in Virginia. He currently lives on the road in his motorhome with his dog/companion, Hamilton (Hammie for short) spreading his MAKING CHOICES philosophy and searching for new actors and coaches, and great stories to develop and put up on the large and small screens.

Watch for the MAKING CHOICES Mobile as it makes its way throughout the country. Who knows... It may be rolling through your town right now. If you see it, come out and say "HI". And if you've got a story to tell, make sure you have it down on a piece of paper. Because you never know...!

For more information on developing your Natural Acting Skills, visit www.beherenownaturally.com

Made in the USA
Middletown, DE
30 September 2023

39822627R00089